T0368365

FINDING
HOPE

IN A HOPELESS WORLD

31-DAY DEVOTIONAL

CONNIE C. SMITHSON

authorHOUSE

AuthorHouse™
1663 Liberty Drive
Bloomington, IN 47403
www.authorhouse.com
Phone: 833-262-8899

Published by AuthorHouse   11/25/2024

ISBN: 979-8-8230-3820-1 (sc)
ISBN: 979-8-8230-3819-5 (e)

Library of Congress Control Number: 2024924421

Print information available on the last page.

Any people depicted in stock imagery provided by Getty Images are models, and such images are being used for illustrative purposes only. Certain stock imagery © *Getty Images.*

This book is printed on acid-free paper.

DEDICATION

This book is dedicated to Rosella Sanders, a mighty woman of God who has stood by me through a lot of hard times. Thank you for being an encouragement to those around you, especially me. Your faithfulness to God and ability to always plant a seed of hope into the lives of others is without a doubt an act of love we could all learn from. I love you big.

Connie

INTRODUCTION

As Christians we live in a dark and dying world. A world filled with turmoil, sadness, and disappointment. Society has become selfish to a degree that seems to be endless. Many people are out for themselves, not giving thought to others around them. Going to the grocery store, our favorite restaurant, or place to shop can be a daunting task.

Trying to maneuver the traffic alone can be stressful, with everyone in a hurry to get from point A to point B, blowing horns, tailgating, and cutting people off in traffic has become the new norm. Then we add to the pile, our daily lives of working, family, church, finances, trying to please everyone, doing everything we can to help others until we have volunteered our time away and find ourselves exhausted and discouraged to the point of no return.

Sometimes we stretch ourselves too thin and we become overwhelmed with all the activities we have committed to, knowing there is no time to get it all done. Having so much on our plates can leave us weighted down and feeling like there is just no hope, all is a loss. Many Christians are living a life of despair and despondency. Let me remind you, that in the middle of everything life throws at us, no matter how big, small, or sad the situation is, there is hope. Hope that is found in a person and his name is Jesus Christ. He is our hope, the one we turn to for strength and help in times of trouble. If you find yourself down and out, and not sure where to turn or who to turn to, it is my prayer that as you read the pages in this book, you find strength to go on, as well as encouragement, and that you look up and turn your face to Jesus— our only living hope.

DAY

1

"These things I have spoken unto you, that in me you might have peace. In the world you shall have tribulation, but be of good cheer, I have overcome the world."

—John 16:33

It is true that we live in a dark world, where corruption seemingly grows every single day. We turn on the news and there is another missing person, another homicide, war raging in the Middle East and here in the United States our freedoms are being threatened daily as they try to push communism down our throats. Our economy has become so unstable that for some, wondering how they will get their next meal has become too real. Why are things so bad? Because we live in a world controlled by Satan and sin. We live in a world where what is wrong is being called right and what is right is being called wrong. Living in this world can be scary, even as Christians. Many Christians are depressed, battling anxiety, stressed out and living a life of fear. It would be easy for me to say, this should not be, but unfortunately it is just as easy to fall into this worlds trap, that Satan sets for us. Satan's goal is to steal our faith, pull us back into the world and away from our Father. It is important that we stay focused on Jesus and remember the price He paid for us at Calvary so that we do not have to walk around with our head down, feeling these negative feelings. Jesus paid a great price for us. Isaiah 53 (KJV) tells us that *"Jesus was despised and rejected of men; a man of sorrows, and acquainted with grief, and we hid as it were our faces from Him; He was despised, and we esteemed him not. (v.4) Surely, He has borne our griefs, and carried our sorrows, yet we did esteem Him stricken, smitten of God, and afflicted. (v.5) He was wounded for our transgressions, He was bruised for our iniquities, the chastisement of our peace was upon Him, and with His stripes we are healed. (v.6) All we like sheep have gone astray; we have turned everyone to his own way, and the Lord has laid on Him the iniquity of us all. (v.7) He was oppressed, and He was afflicted, yet He opened not His mouth. He is brought to the slaughter, and as a sheep before her shearers is dumb, so He opens not His mouth."* Jesus did all of this for us, so that we could live a victorious life. He suffered so that we do not have to. He gave His life for us and after being put in the grave, three days later was raised up. That is our victory! Jesus is our living hope. Because He lives, we live, and we walk in newness of life with Him. When we cannot see a way out or do not know what to do next, when life brings us down, we turn to Him, our blessed hope—Christ Jesus.

MEDITATIONS

_____

_____

_____

_____

_____

_____

_____

_____

_____

_____

_____

_____

_____

_____

DAY

2

"Come unto me, all you who labor and are heavy laden, and I will give you rest."

—John 11-28

Living a victorious life found in Christ Jesus, can be difficult at times, but only because we make it difficult, Often, we are too hard on ourselves. While it is true that we have a responsibility to nurture our relationship with God by praying, praising, and reading the word, we remain in the flesh, therefore we make wrong choices at times. In addition, we will get sick in our bodies, experience fear, and almost daily, we will fight battles brought on by Satan, that we do not have to fight. II Chronicles 20:15-17 (KJV) says *"the battle is not yours, but Gods." "You shall not need to fight in this battle, stand you still, and see the salvation of the Lord with you, O Judah and Jerusalem."* God is fighting for us! All He requires of us is to be still and rest. To enter, into that place of rest, is to enter, into a place where we say *"Lord, I can't, you can."* It is a place where faith comes shining through as we remind ourselves that He is our hope and in Him alone do we place our trust.

Whatever you are dealing with today, picture Jesus standing before you and release it to Him. He is waiting to perform a miracle for you. In Hebrews 6:19 (KJV) Paul said, *"which hope we have as an anchor of the soul, both sure and stedfast."* The hope we find in Jesus is the anchor that holds us.

When tribulation comes your way, grab the anchor, and hold on, let him carry you until the storm passes over. It will pass and soon you will be on the other side, looking back and saying, "look what the Lord, has done!"

MEDITATIONS

_____

_____

_____

_____

_____

_____

_____

_____

_____

_____

_____

_____

_____

DAY

3

"Let us hold fast the profession of our Faith without wavering, for He is faithful who promised."

—Hebrews 10:23

Are you feeling discouraged? Discouragement is something we all deal with and it comes from various sources—being disappointed by someone, failing to accomplish all that we think we should, setting goals for ourselves that are not realistic or perhaps we tried pursuing something that was never Gods will for us.

It is during these times; we must choose to put our hope in God and let Him sustain us. If you find yourself feeling overwhelmed, seek Gods word. It is in His word that we are reminded of His faithfulness and promises. You can also call on the Lord, He will hear you when you cry out to Him. In Psalms 18:6 (KJV) David said, *"In my distress I called upon the Lord, and cried unto my God, he heard my voice out of his temple, and my cry came before him, even unto his ears."* As we place our hope in God our thinking will shift. We get our focus off our problems and onto the one who changes everything.

If you feel discouraged today cry out to God and listen for His voice, trust Him, and know that He has only the best for you. Romans 8:28 says, *"And we know that all things work together for good to them who love God, to them who are the called according to His purpose."* God is working all things together for your good. Stay grounded in Him and be expecting. The best is yet to come in your life. You are just getting started.

MEDITATIONS

_____

_____

_____

_____

_____

_____

_____

_____

_____

_____

_____

_____

_____

_____

DAY

4

"Jesus said unto him, if you can believe, all things are possible to him who believes."

—Mark 9:23

Hanging over my bed is a canvas with the engraving that says, *"It always seems impossible until it's done."* We often look at our circumstances, what we are going through as an impossible situation, meaning we do not know what to do and in all actuality, there is nothing we can do to resolve it. We may try and try again only to achieve the same outcome—failure. So, what do we do in times like this? Unfortunately, most get caught in a cycle of continuing to try and failing.

I have been there myself. We get exhausted with the battle we are fighting and eventually find ourselves without the strength to put forth effort to simply try again. Here is the good news, once you have reached that point, you have arrived too the place God wants you to be. You now need to make the decision to become totally dependent on God.

It may seem like all hope is lost, but it is not. As long as you remain in relationship with God, you have one standing with you, who you can place your hope in. Communicate with your Heavenly Father and tell Him you recognize there is nothing you can do, acknowledge to Him that He alone is your only hope. He will faithfully, step into your situation and turn the impossible to possible, because with God—all things are possible!

MEDITATIONS

_____

_____

_____

_____

_____

_____

_____

_____

_____

_____

_____

_____

_____

DAY

5

"I will never leave you, Nor forsake you. So that we may boldly say, the Lord is my helper, and I will not fear what man shall do unto me."

—Hebrews 13:5-6

I recently heard a song that contains the lyrics, *"Even when it looks hopeless, I will continue to trust, He will never leave my side."* When you are going through a difficult time and it seems as though everything you do only makes the situation worse or maybe it's a circumstance where you have prayed and prayed, left it in God's hands, but He still has not answered. You may question where God is in all of it. Be encouraged today and understand that God does hear you, God sees your desperation and He is in the middle of it all. He promises to never leave us nor forsake us.

In Isaiah 43:2 (KJV) He says *"when you pass through the*

waters, I will be with you; and through the rivers, they shall not overflow you: when you walk through the fire, you shall not be burned; either shall the flame kindle upon you."

This is one of His many promises to us. In this scripture He promises that when hardship comes our way, He is with us. When the difficulty you're facing seems to be getting worse, rather than better, He is walking with you, He is the one who makes a way when you cannot see a way, all He ask is that you trust Him.

When family, friends, your pastor, and money cannot fix the problem—trust him. He will bring closure. He will answer your hearts cry. The answer may not always be the one you were expecting, but you can rest assure, it will be what is in your best interest—Trust Him—only trust Him.

MEDITATIONS

DAY

6

"For I the Lord your God will hold your right hand, saying unto you, Fear not; I will help you."

—Isaiah 41:13

Fear according to the world's definition is "an unpleasant emotion caused by the belief that someone or something is dangerous, likely to cause pain or a threat." Fear causes feeling of anxiousness, as the person feels threatened by someone or something. Sometimes fear is brought on by a consequence for a wrong action. In Genesis 3:10 (KJV) Adam said, "I heard your voice in the garden, and I was afraid, because I was naked; and I hid myself." Adam had sinned against God and quickly recognized the effect of his sin, causing him to fear as he was about to answer to God for what he had done.

The causes of fear can be endless, some people fear things such as death, change, the dark, storms, insects, the unknown etc., then there are those people who fear everything. They are labeled by the world as having panophobia. As a child of God we should have a "healthy fear" about things that can cause us harm, but we should not be walking bound to a spirit of fear that can hold us back, keeping us from moving forward into all that God has for us.

To walk in fear is to not trust God, it displays a lack of faith, and it is not pleasing to God. I John 4:18 (KJV) says, *"there is no fear in love; but perfect love cast out fear: because fear has torment. He that fears is not made perfect in love."* If you are struggling with fear in your life, ask God to remove it, to deliver you from all fear, to fill you with his peace that surpasses all understanding. Jesus wore a crown of thorns on His head as He was tormented at Calvary, so that you do not have to live a life of fear but one of peace. John 14:27 (KJV) says, *"peace I leave with you, my peace I give unto you; not as the world gives, give I unto you. Let not your heart be troubled, neither let it be afraid."*

It is my prayer that God bless you with His peace today and help you to walk in the freedom made possible by the cross and what Jesus there did.

MEDITATIONS

_____

_____

_____

_____

_____

_____

_____

_____

_____

_____

_____

_____

_____

_____

DAY

7

"I will lift up my eyes unto the hills, from where comes my help."

—Psalms 121:1

What are your eyes fixed on today? I once knew a young lady who stayed in a state of distress. She worried about everything, even those things that had not yet happened. When trouble came her way, she dwelt on it and cried over it, she had no peace. Eventually, she developed physical ailments that could only be explained by her doctors, as the stress in her life being the cause. This lady's eyes were on her circumstances, and herself.

The word tells us to lift up our eyes—look up. In essence, it is saying, do not walk around with your head down, feeling sorry for yourself—look up! Look up to the one who made Heaven and Earth, Look up to the Lord, He is where your help comes from. The 121st Psalm goes on to say, *"He will not suffer our foot to be moved: He who keeps you will not slumber."* (v.3) He neither slumbers nor sleeps. He is your keeper. He will preserve you from all evil. In Isaiah 40:26 (KJV) it says, *"Lift up your eyes on high, and behold who has created these things, that brings out their host by number. He calls them all by names by the greatness of His might, for that He is strong in power; not one fails."*

He is the creator of this world, the one who named every star in the celestial. The one who created you and knows all things. This is who we are to look up to. Focus on the problem solver—not the problem. He alone is all power and able to do all things. Ephesians 3:20 says, *"Who is able to do exceeding, abundantly above all that we ask or think."* His ways and His thoughts are higher than ours. Look up, not down, behind you, or even in front of you at what may or may not be, but rather look to the one who is carrying you. He has a plan, and He is working to bring that plan for your life to fruition. Keep looking up to your Father, today could be your day of breakthrough, the day that suddenly moment happens for you. Look up with expectancy. Today, just may be your day!

MEDITATIONS

_____

_____

_____

_____

_____

_____

_____

_____

_____

_____

_____

_____

_____

_____

DAY

8

"He gives power to the faint; and to them who have no might He increases strength."

—Isaiah 40:29

We can all become weary at times. Weariness comes in the form of physical, spiritual, and emotional. In todays terminology we hear it referred to as being "burnt out." It is easy to reach that place of weariness with all that we have going on in our lives. Daily task like work, school, church, and family can all lead to weariness. As much as God is with us in our good times, He is also, just as much with us in our times of weariness.

Hope is Gods antidote to weariness. In Isaiah 40:31 (KJV) it says, *"But they who wait upon the Lord shall renew their strength; they shall mount up with wings as eagles, they shall run, and not be weary, they shall walk, and not faint."* This is Gods promise, to give us strength when we grow weary.

He gives strength to those who are weak. He supernaturally increases faith, and enlarges our views, so that we may once again see the goodness of the Lord all around us.

In II Corinthians 12:10 (KJV) Paul said, *"Therefore I take pleasure in infirmities, in reproaches, in necessities, in persecutions, in distresses for Christ's sake: for when I am weak, then am I strong."* Paul is saying when I know I am weak, then the strength of Christ can be exhibited through me. The same holds true for us. Once we come to the end of ourselves, feel like we cannot take another step, like we are paralyzed to some degree, it is then, that God can step in and supernaturally do a work in us.

If you are feeling weary today, lay at the feet of Jesus and let Him strengthen and restore you as only He can do.

MEDITATIONS

_____

_____

_____

_____

_____

_____

_____

_____

_____

_____

_____

_____

_____

_____

DAY

9

"And lest I should be exalted above measure through the abundance of the Revelations, there was given to me a thorn in the flesh."

—II Corinthians 12:7

The Apostle Paul in this passage of scripture and throughout was dealing with a specific issue that was causing him great problems. The word does not tell us what Paul's thorn was, but alludes to it being extremely difficult, to the point, it seemed as though, Satan was trying to take him out.

Paul prayed three times for God to deliver him from the infirmity, but God simply said, *"my grace is sufficient."* As a Christian we are never told that trouble will not come our way, as a matter of fact, it is the exact opposite. We are told to expect trouble and given instruction for what to do when circumstances in our life, seem to be spiraling out of control. We endure, and go through, with God allowing certain things to happen as an impediment to keep us crying out to Him.

We often seek God, asking Him over and over to move in our circumstances, to answer our prayers and set us free from the thorn that seems to be choking the life out of us. God in His wisdom knows best. At times we question God, asking Him, why? Sometimes we wonder if God has heard our prayers or if He is just ignoring us, and then there are those occasions we cry out in desperation, and God responds with, *"my grace is sufficient child."*

What we must understand is that God is keeping us humble before Him. God is more concerned about our spirit man than our flesh, and so, He is going to allow whatever it takes to keep us before Him, putting Him first, and seeking His will. If his answer continues to be a flat no, then we must trust Him, and know that what He has purposed for our life, far outweighs and is above anything we could ever ask or think. Be encouraged today to accept Gods no to your thorn being removed and understand that his grace truly is sufficient.

MEDITATIONS

DAY
10

"For God so loved the world that He gave His only begotten son, that whosoever believes in Him should not perish, but have everlasting life."

—John 3:16

Gods love for us is one of His greatest attributes. It was His love for us that carried Him down a long dusty road, to an old rugged cross. God Himself took on flesh—living, dying, and resurrecting to life again, to demonstrate the extent of His love for us. King David referred to God's love as being too marvelous for his understanding. (Psalms 139:6)

Paul in Ephesians 3:17-19 (KJV) said, *"That Christ may dwell in your hearts by Faith; that you, being rooted and grounded in love may be able to comprehend with all saints what is the breadth, and length, and depth and height; and to know the love of Christ, which passes knowledge, that you might be filled with all the fulness of God."* Gods love for us extends farther than we can comprehend in this finite mind. His love is by far, the deepest, most powerful love we will ever experience. His word tells us that He, Himself is love.

I John 4:8 (KJV) says, *"Anyone who does not love does not know God, because God is love."* We say that we love God and I believe we show God our love through the way we live, our obedience to Him, the way we worship Him and spend time in relationship with Him. However, in all that we do to prove our love for God, it does not compare to His everlasting love for us. If you find yourself in a place today, where you feel unloved by those around you, remember there is one who loves you so much, that He gave His life for you and His name is Jesus. His love is unconditional, limitless, and it awaits you, if you will only seek Him with your whole heart. Jesus loves you!

MEDITATIONS

_____

_____

_____

_____

_____

_____

_____

_____

_____

_____

_____

_____

_____

_____

DAY

11

"Praise you the Lord. Praise God in His sanctuary: Praise Him in the firmament of His power."

—Psalms 150:1

As children of God there is one thing we can be assured of, Satan has a strategic attack planned against us—a plan to break our Faith. There are a number of ways, in which he comes at us, but perhaps the most effective is, within our mind. What we think on, whether positive or negative, has a direct impact on our heart. Satan will engage us in battle by bringing up our past sins and failures. Oftentimes, we are the ones who furnish him with the ammunition to attack us, by means of the words we speak, what we watch on television, what we listen to on the radio and even the company we keep. There are people in our lives, be it family or friends, who cannot wait for the opportunity to bring up our past, reminding us of who we were prior to our salvation experience—yes, Satan uses other people, to successfully catapult an attack. So, how do we stop Satan in his tracks? How do we overpower him and send him packing? Erupt in praise! Open your mouth, begin to give God glory for all that He has brought you through, for His blessings in your life, and for who He is.

Meditate on His word and remember His promises, that are Yes and Amen. Philippians 4:8 (KJV) says, *"Finally brethren, whatsoever things are true, whatsoever things are honest, whatsoever things are just, whatsoever things are pure, whatsoever things are lovely, whatsoever things are of good report; If there be any virtue and if there be any praise, think on these things."* Our God is worthy of all praise, all glory and all honor. Praise Him today in all that you are confronted with and watch as the enemy flees in defeat, with nowhere to run, but back to the pit of Hell where he originated. Praise ye the Lord!

MEDITATIONS

DAY

12

"This I recall to my mind, Therefore have I hope.

—Lamentations 3:21

We can all look back and remember a time when we were in a valley, a place of decrease, sickness, spiritual dryness, trouble in our family, a friend that may have forsaken us or perhaps the ministry we were involved in, fell apart overnight. A valley—a dark place, a place everything appeared hopeless. For some of you, you may currently be in a valley. I think if we were to be honest, we could all say, yes, I am walking through a valley.

As a Christian and being called by God to fulfill what He has assigned to us, does not exempt us from walking through the valley of the shadow of death and experiencing days of hopelessness. David was anointed to be King of Israel, yet he finds himself fleeing for his life and ultimately hiding in the cave of Adullam. Joseph went from wearing the coat of many colors to garments of a slave, and a prisoner. He went from the comfort of his father's house, to a dungeon.

Moses spent forty years in the desert as a shepherd. Jeremiah in Lamentations three is living in despair. He would say, *"I am a man who has seen affliction by the rod of His wrath."* (V.1) *"He has led me and brought me into the darkness, but not into light."* (v.2) *"Surely against me He has turned."* (v.3) *"My flesh and my skin has he made old; He has broken my bones."* (v.4)

"He has built against me and compassed me with gall and travail." (v.5) *"He has set me in dark places, as they that be dead of old."* (v.6) *"He has hedged me about, that I cannot get out: He has made my chain heavy."* (v.7) *"Also when I cry and shout, He shuts out my prayer."* (v.8) In all of these verses you can hear the brokenness, hopelessness, and feel Jeremiahs pain, but then in verse twenty-one, Jeremiah says, *"This I recall to mind, therefore have I hope."* It is as if he suddenly remembers Gods promises of mercy and grace and his hope is restored. Whatever valley you find yourself in today, stop and remember Gods promise to you, stand on His word and trust that He is working to take you from the valley to the mountain top.

MEDITATIONS

_____

_____

_____

_____

_____

_____

_____

_____

_____

_____

_____

_____

_____

DAY

13

"But they who wait upon the lord shall renew their strength; they shall mount up with wings as eagles; they shall run, and not be weary; they shall walk and not faint."

—Isaiah 40:31

There are times in our lives where we go through a period of waiting on God. It has been said that this is the most difficult position to find oneself—waiting on God. We live in a fast pace society where everything must be done at the moment we expect it, and to our liking. This is not how God operates. God is not on our time—we are on His. Waiting on God to come through in our situations, did not just begin with us. We can draw encouragement from faithful followers in the Bible, such as, Abraham and Sarah. They waited years for the birth of their promised son Isaac; Moses was in the desert leading the Israelites for forty years; David waited fifteen years to take the throne after being anointed by God; Joseph was in prison for thirteen years before being set free and put on the throne. I am sure that during their wait they became weary and grew discouraged at times, just as we do.

Often it feels as though God has forgotten us, we may even question whether what God promised us was Him or coming from our own desires. It is easy to grow weary, but Isaiah tells us that, *"They who wait upon the Lord will have renewed strength they shall run, and not be weary; and they shall walk and not faint."*

In the waiting, God sees what we are dealing with, He hears our cries, He is closely watching the events of our life as they unfold, and He is in control of it all. He has not forgotten you, most likely He is teaching you and preparing you for greater things. Keep your focus on Him and wait with patience—The best is yet to come!

MEDITATIONS

_____

_____

_____

_____

_____

_____

_____

_____

_____

_____

_____

_____

_____

_____

DAY

14

"And the Lord said unto Satan, have you considered my servant Job, that there is none like him in the Earth, a perfect and upright man, one who fears God, and eschews evil?"

—Job 1:8

As it was with Job, so has it been with every Christian at some point in their walk with God—we have all been put to the test. Fortunately, for us, the tests we endure are not to the degree Job walked through. Job's faith was tested greatly, but he never wavered. While there are many lessons to be learned from Job's experience, I believe the main lesson is to never give up.

Job maintained his faith in God, he never gave up on life, or God. No matter how hopeless your circumstance may seem, in Christ you have hope, in Christ you are victorious. There are going to be times in life, when we go through a test that requires us to stand and fight, a time when friends and family give up and think we are crazy to continue believing for something that seems impossible.

Jobs own wife told him to curse God and die, his friends questioned him, asking what actions he committed that would cause him such great suffering. Job was a faithful servant of God—a man of great faith. Never has a man been tested like Job and withstood the horror he went through, but Jobs faith remained, he did not curse God, he knew God would bring him out and when the test was over for Job, God not only brought him out, but rewarded him with double for what he had lost.

Job unleashed his faith, taking it to another level. God is waiting to do the same for us in our time of testing. His word tells us in the book of Hebrews that He is the same yesterday, today, and forever. What He did for Job, He will do for us. When test come our way, no matter the test we should always ask God what He wants us to learn. God has a redemptive plan, no matter what we lose in the process, we must not despair, instead we need to be like Job—unleash great faith, wait for God to deliver us, and bring us into a new dimension of his goodness. Be encouraged today to keep holding on to Gods hand of security, keep the faith and trust Him to bring you out of the execrable time you find yourself in.

MEDITATIONS

DAY

15

"And the Lord said, I have surely seen the affliction of my people which are in Egypt and have heard their cry by reason of their taskmasters; for I know their sorrows."

—Exodus 3:7

The children of Israel faced many afflictions. As God's children we are not free from the pain and sorrow this life can bring. Scripture tells us that it rains on the just and the unjust. (Matthew 5:45) Every trial that comes our way as a child of God is either caused or allowed by Him for a purpose. There are many reasons for why God allows it to "rain on the just." For instance, when things are going well for us, we do not always pray the way we do when we are in the wilderness. God wants to hear from us constantly and at times He wants us quiet so we can hear from Him. God desires a relationship with us and like all relationships, it requires talking and listening. Another reason God allows affliction, is to test our faith. God wants to teach us dependence on him, He wants to show us His provision as we go through, so by teaching us dependence and showing us how He will provide, our faith is built.

At times, God allows affliction in our lives to prepare us for the call He has on our life. God wants to move us from our comfort zone, remove all things including some people from our life, that may be hindering what He is trying to accomplish through us. He breaks us down, to build us back up into being all that He wants us to be. Finally, God allows affliction to see how we will respond. He allows things to get as bad as they can, to show us our weakness. What is in us will ultimately come out of us, and while God knows what is on the inside of us, we do not always know. He allows the affliction to intensify, and when it does, we see things like, envy, jealousy, bitterness, hate, resentment, selfishness, and unforgiveness come to the surface.

Once we recognize the "junk" that is not of God, then we can turn to God for deliverance and He shows us his delivering power. What is afflicting you today? More important, what is God trying to reveal to you through the affliction?

MEDITATIONS

_____

_____

_____

_____

_____

_____

_____

_____

_____

_____

_____

_____

_____

DAY

16

"For all the promises of God In him are yea, and in him Amen, unto the Glory of God by us."

—II Corinthians 1:20

There will come a time in the believer's life when God makes them a specific promise and then sets them aside and carries them through a time of preparation. Gods promise to every believer is Yes and Amen, however, that does not mean the believer is immediately ready to receive the promise. Often, preparation is deemed necessary by God. You may ask, what does the preparation process look like? It is different for each individual person and designed by God for a purpose specific to their need. Preparation includes pruning away some dead branches, allowing many tests, followed by waiting, and of course, the attacks of the enemy. The enemy's job is to block the blessing and to try and deter the believer—to keep the promise from coming forth. Everyone has a place where they are comfortable, moving out of that place of comfort can be scary. If the enemy is successful, fear of the unknown will keep the believer in a stationary position, so that moving forward is not an option.

The enemy may even take the believer in a direction that was never intended by God. In addition, the enemy will send distractions to turn the believer's attention away from the promise, and on to something irrelevant, thereby, showing the believer a way to obtain the promise that is not God's way or a part of Gods plan, such was the case with Abraham and Sarah.

The preparation process is often slow and there will be opposition, and as stated a long wait. I, myself, have been going through the preparation process for more than seven years now, and I can tell you, I have experienced every single detail I mentioned. It is important to learn, to let the dead branches fall, keep your focus on God and His promise to you. Keep your Faith grounded in the God of hope, knowing that as you go through the process, the promise maker is also the promise keeper. You will come out victorious having obtained the promise tailored just for you.

MEDITATIONS

_____

_____

_____

_____

_____

_____

_____

_____

_____

_____

_____

_____

_____

_____

_____

DAY

17

"And the people murmured against Moses, saying what shall we drink? And he cried unto the Lord; and the Lord showed him a tree, which when he had cast into the waters, the waters were made sweet."

—Exodus 15:22-25

The Lord showed Moses a tree, which was a type of the cross. When Moses grabbed the tree and put it into the bitter water of Marah, they were made sweet. It was out of obedience to what the Lord was telling Moses to do and by Faith that Moses grabbed the tree and cast it into the water. First came the problem, then came obedience, which followed an expression of Faith and then came the victory. If Moses had just looked at the tree and not grabbed it the water would not have been made sweet and there would have been no victory. Likewise, when we are presented with a problem, God wants us to by Faith, be obedient to the leading of the Holy Spirit in our circumstances and grab the tree, so we to, can experience victory in our lives. We, like the children of Israel tend to forget where God brought us from and what He has already brought us through.

We resort to murmuring and complaining, just like the children of Israel. As you face the trials and tribulation of life, grab the tree, go back to the cross, where the one who died for you, made it possible for you to come walking out of the fire without even the smell of smoke on you. He is the way, the truth and life. In him alone is hope found to keep going until you reach the other side.

MEDITATIONS

_____

_____

_____

_____

_____

_____

_____

_____

_____

_____

_____

_____

_____

_____

DAY

18

"Weeping may endure for a night, but joy comes in the morning."

—Psalms 30:5

There are no more comforting and hopeful words than those found in Psalm 30:5. It is a verse that can help you up when you are down, and carry you as you go through difficult times. When life is painful, and the emotional struggle is great, it brings solace to the soul. It is a reminder that we are not alone, the heaviness we feel today will be gone tomorrow.

This does not mean tomorrow, as in the next day because it may carry over for many days to come, but it does mean that your tomorrow is coming. You will not be where you are now, forever. Eventually, your morning is coming. We have the hope of a new day. Our circumstances may go unchanged, but we have Gods promise of bringing joy in the middle of it all. Suffering is a reality, but God promises restoration. Gods word tells us that his joy is our strength. (Neh.8:10) James tells us, *"to count it all joy when you fall into divers temptations."* Why? Because *"the trying of your faith works patience."* (v.3) David said, *"Therefore my heart is glad, and my glory rejoices: my flesh also rest in hope."* (Psalm16:9 KJV) In the difficult times of life, as well as, the good, if we will only rest in the Lord Jesus Christ, knowing He has the ability to bring us out of any circumstance and will eventually do so, then we will have joy, we will be strengthened and we will have a renewed hope only found in Him.

Be encouraged today in knowing that while this day may look grim and full of trouble, tomorrow is coming and with the dawning of a new day, comes the joy of the Lord, just for you.

MEDITATIONS

DAY

19

Psalms 91

"He who dwells in the secret place of the most High shall abide under the shadow of the Almighty. (v.1) KJV

I will say of the Lord, He is my refuge and my Fortress: My God in Him will I trust. (v.2) KJV

Surely He shall deliver you from the snare of the fowler, and from the noisome pestilence. (v.3) KJV

He shall cover you with His feathers, and under His wings shall you trust: His truth shall be your shield and buckler. (v.4) KJV

You shall not be afraid for the terror by night; nor the arrow that flies by day. (v.5) KJV

Nor for the pestilence that walks in darkness; nor for the destruction that wastes at noonday. (v.6) KJV

A thousand shall fall at your side, and ten thousand at your right hand; but it shall not come near you. (v.7) KJV

Only with your eyes shall you behold and see the reward of the wicked. (v.8) KJV

Because you have made the Lord, who is my Refuge, even the most High, your Habitation. (v.9) KJV

There shall no evil befall you, neither shall any plague come near your dwelling. (v.10) KJV

For He shall give His angels charge over you, to keep you in all your ways. (v.11) KJV

They shall bear you up in their hands, lest you dash your foot against a stone. (v.12) KJV

You shall tread upon the lion and adder: the young lion and the dragon shall you trample under feet. (v.13) KJV

Because he has set his love upon me, therefore will I deliver him: I will set him on high, because he has known my name. (v.14) KJV

He shall call upon me, and I will answer him: I will be with him in trouble, I will deliver him, and honour him. (v.15) KJV

With long life will I satisfy him, and show him my Salvation." (v.16) KJV

MEDITATIONS

DAY

20

"And God said, Let there be light."

—Genesis 1:3

When God speaks everything changes. All He does is speak the word and breakthrough happens. The words of God are so profound that He spoke the world into existence. He said, *"let there be light,"* and everything changed as light came forth. The same voice that spoke the world into existence is the same voice that speaks to us. At times He may not speak directly to us, but speak to our circumstances, and when He does, they turn around. Throughout the Bible we read about God speaking and situations changing.

In John 11, Lazarus had been dead for four days and scripture says, Jesus spoke with a loud voice commanding him to come forth and he came up out of the grave. (v.43) KJV In Luke 7, the widows only son had died and when Jesus arrived, He spoke to the boy saying, *"young man, I say unto you, Arise."* And he who was dead sat up and began to speak. (v.15) KJV In Mark 4, the disciples, along with Jesus, were in a ship when a great storm of wind, and waves began to beat into the ship. Jesus being asleep was awakened by the disciples who were fearful and concerned that Jesus did not care about the circumstances surrounding them, as that during the storm He remained sleeping.

Once He was awake, Jesus spoke to the storm saying, *"peace, be still."* And there was a great calm, as they continued their journey to the shore. This is a perfect example of how we should be as we go through the storms of life—resting and trusting God. Just as He spoke to the natural storm in Mark, He will speak to your circumstances and they will change.

No matter what you are up against today, look to God, surrender it all to Him and when resolution comes, know that your Father—creator of the universe, the one who heals, raises, and delivers— has spoken.

MEDITATIONS

_____

_____

_____

_____

_____

_____

_____

_____

_____

_____

_____

_____

_____

DAY

21

"And the rain descended, and the floods came, and the winds blew, and beat upon the house; and it fell not for it was founded upon a rock."

—Matthew 7:25

Rocks in a physical state are constantly being formed, worn down and formed again. This process is called weathering. Once a rock has been broken down erosion begins transporting the bits of rocks and minerals away. It takes thousands of years for rocks to change, but they do change. Some of the activity that causes the change is events such as, rushing water, like that of rivers found moving quickly in the mountains, strong waves on the ocean shore, the freeze/thaw cycle that causes mountains to crumble over time, as large rocks breakdown into little rocks and finally, wind. Wind can carry bits of sand and grit and blast away layers of rock. We can be likened to a physical rock.

If we are standing on the wrong foundation with our faith anchored in everything, but Jesus, when the storms of life come our way, when we get that unexpected phone call that brings devasting news, we will be like the physical rock and crumble. However, when our foundation is "the rock"—Christ Jesus, then and only then are we grounded, in such a way, that when the test and trials come rushing in, it will not seem so overwhelming that we cannot bear it.

David in Psalm 40 said, *"He brought me up also out of an horrible pit, out of the miry clay, and set my feet upon a rock and established my goings."* (v.2) KJV In Psalm 61, David said, *"From the end of the Earth will I cry unto you, when my heart is overwhelmed: lead me to the rock that is higher than I."* (v.2) KJV David stood on the rock that will not crumble, The Rock—Christ Jesus. What are you standing on? What is your foundation?

MEDITATIONS

_____

_____

_____

_____

_____

_____

_____

_____

_____

_____

_____

_____

_____

_____

DAY

22

*"The Lord will give strength unto his people;
the Lord will bless his people with peace."*

—Psalms 29:11

One Sunday morning during our morning worship service, the Lord gave my pastor a word for the congregation and that word was "GET UP!" How do we "get up" when the troubles of this life are weighing us down? How do we "get up" when things like depression, anxiety, addiction, broken relationships, financial burdens, poor health, and difficulties on the job are binding, seemingly refusing to let go, no matter our efforts? How do we "get up?"

We "get up" by exchanging our efforts for God's strength. We must learn to maintain our faith in Christ Jesus. He alone is our strength, refuge, help and peace. David said in Psalm 138, *"Though I walk in the midst of trouble, you will revive me: you shall stretch forth your hand against the wrath of my enemies and your right hand shall save me."* (v.7) KJV

Jesus defeated every trouble we come against today, at Calvary's cross of yesterday. Whatever you are struggling with, no matter how significant or insignificant it may seem, release it to your Heavenly Father. He is faithful to perform His word and fulfill His promises to us. He is our restorer and our hope—He is our strength. Therefore, we can "get up" because He is waiting to pick us up and carry us through this journey, we call life. Be encouraged today to take His hand and "GET UP!" You are not in this alone.

MEDITATIONS

DAY

23

"That was the true light, which lighteth every man who comes into the world."

—John 1:9

There are many lights in this dark world, but there is only one true light—Christ Jesus. As a child of God, we can all think back over our lives and remember the moments when the "true light" was there guiding us, as we wandered through the darkness. God can seem far away when the darkness blankets us. However, the truth is, He is never far at all. He is with us, always. When we stumble, He is there to catch us, when we make a mess, He is there to clean it up, when we fall, He picks us up, when we have a need, He provides, when sickness comes, He is our healer, when division tries to invade our relationships, He raises up a standard against the enemy, sustains us, and brings unity, when our enemies come against us, He is our vindicator, when the storms of life come and our faith grows weak, He holds us up on the water, so we do not sink, when we fail, He loves us and shows us His compassion, when we are sad, He brings us joy, when we feel lonely, He is by our side whispering, *"I will never leave you, nor forsake you."* When anxiety tries to move in, He takes our thoughts captive and brings them into obedience with Him. He gives us peace and teaches us to rest. When we lose someone close to us to death, He is our comfort, when we have no one to turn to, nowhere to go, and need an answer to questions about circumstances out of our control, He points us to His word, He gives us wisdom and makes a way out. When we pray until exhaustion sets in and we cannot find the words or strength to go on, He sends someone to pray with us and for us.

When life happens and our world is spinning out of control, He is a beam of light that will never dim or burn out. He is all that we need, as we travel through the dark paths of life—He is the "True Light."

MEDITATIONS

_____

_____

_____

_____

_____

_____

_____

_____

_____

_____

_____

_____

_____

_____

DAY

24

"Take therefore no thought for tomorrow: for tomorrow shall take thought for the things of itself. Sufficient unto the day is the evil thereof."

—Matthew 6:34

We all at times tend to get caught up in the worries of tomorrow. We often focus on what is going to be, what could be, and what is next for our future, more so, than getting through the one day standing before us. What if tomorrow doesn't come? What did you do today? We all have choices to make, and our choices determine our outcome. We can praise, pray, and trust God to provide for us today or we can sit, worrying about all that lies ahead of us.

In the flesh, we think things like, what are we going to eat for dinner? What are we going to wear? For some, it may be the out of town business trip scheduled or if you are a parent, how you are going to get your child to their next practice or game. We pull out our trusty calendars and plan, writing things down to help organize our busy days and weeks to come, but What if tomorrow doesn't come? What did you do today?

Did you help someone in need? Did you laugh and make the best out of a bad situation? Did you take the time to give an encouraging word to someone? Or were you too focused on tomorrow and what is about to surface in your own life?

The things in life that do not matter—matter to us, and the things that should matter—do not. There comes a time, when we need to sit back, get alone with God, forget about tomorrow, and simply trust Him to provide and bring us through today. We get bombarded by the craziness of this world and are so incredibly busy that most people today, spend more time away from home than they do at home. Life is busy and hard, time is passing by, and within a matter of seconds our entire life can be turned upside down. We never know when the moment will come, that we exhale our last breath, it could be today, if it is, tomorrow does not matter. The only thing that matters is that we are in right standing with God. Are you saved? Do you know the Lord Jesus Christ as your savior? If not, make today your day, step into relationship with Him. Do not put off until tomorrow, what you can do now.

Step into a new life, cast your cares upon Him and do not worry about tomorrow, it may not come, and if it doesn't, what did you do today?

MEDITATIONS

DAY

25

"He said to me, "Son of man, can these bones live?" And I answered, "O Lord God, you know.""

—Ezekiel 37:3

Have you ever been in a place of spiritual dryness? You try praying and the words will not come, you attempt to read the word or worship and find yourself, staring into space, thinking about all that you have going on in your life, rather than spending time with God. I have experienced this a few times during my Christian walk, and I always ask, why? I think there are many reasons for why as a Christian we have, what often is described as, a "desert like experience."

Sometimes, it is because we have yielded to a particular sin in our life, but more often I believe, we get too busy. We may skip a day of prayer and worshipping God as well as reading the word, because we did not have time. I have always heard that when you are too busy for God—you are just too busy.

It could be that God wants to get us quiet and listening, so He can speak, and we can hear. Thankfully, God always meets us where we are. A spiritual dry place for me seldom last longer than two or three days. I am sure we have all encountered this at one time or another, but what about a spiritual coma? I would have to say this is much different. Spiritual coma is a term I have coined to describe someone who is backslidden, meaning, they have stopped praying, praising, attending church services, reading the word, and are slowly slipping back into their old ways, prior to getting saved.

If that sounds like you, you my friend, are in trouble and need to come back to the Lord. God is waiting for you with open arms. The only thing you need to do is first, ask Him for forgiveness, next, start thanking Him for forgiving you, begin to worship Him and make time for Him, putting Him first in your life. Come back to your first love, drink of the living water, and everything that is dry or comatose in your life will be restored, as spiritual death gives way to life found only in Christ Jesus.

MEDITATIONS

DAY

26

"Come now, and let us reason together, says the Lord: though your sins be as scarlet, they shall be white as snow."

—Isaiah 1:8

During the Winter, the flowers cease to bloom, the grass loses its beautiful green color as it converts over to brown, the trees have shed their leaves and stand bare. All the life and colorfulness of Spring and Summer dissipate. However, when a fresh snow falls, it covers the flowers, grass, and trees transforming them into something beautiful once again. Likewise, when a lost sinner comes to Christ he or she is spiritually dead, but the moment they surrender their life to Jesus a transformation takes place and that which was dead, cursed by the bondage of sin, takes on a look of beauty. The red blood of Jesus does for man, what the white snow of Winter does for the flowers, grass, and trees—it transforms.

It takes what was once dead and makes it beautiful. The snow will fade away as it melts and the flowers, grass, and trees will return to their original state, but with Jesus the conversion that takes place in mans heart is permanent, it will not melt away like the snow—Jesus comes to stay.

If you do not know Jesus as your Savior, once again I plead with you to invite Him into your heart. Trade your darkness for light and be supernaturally transformed by the power of God. It will be the best decision you ever make and one that will never bring you regret.

MEDITATIONS

DAY

27

"And they came unto Him, bringing one sick of the palsy, which was borne of four. And when they could not come near unto Him for the press, they uncovered the roof where He was: and when they had broken it up, they let down the bed wherein the sick of the palsy lay. When Jesus saw their faith, He said unto the sick of the palsy, son, thy sins be forgiven thee."

—Mark 2:3-5

Feel like giving up and quitting? In this scripture Jesus had just returned to Capernaum after weeks of ministering around the area of Galilee. Arriving at the home of Peter, one of His soon to be disciples, noise of His return spread throughout the city, resulting in hundreds of people descending to Peter's home, filling it to capacity.

In the crowd was a man who had been paralyzed for

many years, lying on a cot. This man was unable to move and do for himself and as a result, he was dependent on others for everything he needed. He was not only afflicted in his physical body, but spiritually he was without God.

Depending on those helping him to move him from place to place, after he, as well as, the men carrying him, heard that Jesus was in the city, the men did all they could to get their paralyzed friend to Jesus so he could receive his miracle, believe and get saved. These men stopped at nothing to get their friend to Jesus and when they could not get through the crowd and the press, they managed to get him to the top of the house, remove the roof and lower him down.

The men faced an impossible situation and they could have given up but did not. They were determined to get their friend to Jesus, and they did. Be encouraged today not to give up. No matter what problems you have or how impossible it may seem to you, stay focused on your source of hope—Jesus. Let your determination keep you pressing on in your walk with God and stay in the fight, your day of victory is coming!

MEDITATIONS

_____

_____

_____

_____

_____

_____

_____

_____

_____

_____

_____

_____

_____

_____

DAY
28

"And He opened His mouth and taught them saying."

—Matthew 5:2

This scripture is the introduction of the teachings of Jesus in the sermon on the mount and is where the Beatitudes begin. Starting with verse number three Jesus taught, *"Blessed are the poor in Spirit for theirs is the kingdom of Heaven. Blessed are they who mourn: for they shall be comforted. Blessed are the meek: for they shall inherit the Earth. Blessed are they which do hunger and thirst after Righteousness: for they shall be filled. Blessed are the merciful: for they shall obtain mercy. Blessed are the pure in heart: for they shall see God. Blessed are the peacemakers: for they shall be called children of God. Blessed are they which are persecuted for Righteousness sake: for theirs is the kingdom of Heaven. Blessed are you, when men shall revile you, and persecute you, and shall say all manner of evil against you falsely, for my sake. Rejoice, and be exceeding glad: for great is your reward in Heaven: for so persecuted they the prophets which were before you."* (vs. 4-12 KJV)

The Beatitudes teach that we will be blessed even in difficult times, what a promise our Father gives. As we go through each day, if we will only exemplify the qualities Jesus taught—we will be blessed. I pray reading the Beatitudes will challenge you to be more Christ-like and, also be a reminder that no matter what obstacles come your way in this life, you will be blessed! Not only blessed, but blessed beyond measure as you, *"Let your light shine before men, that they may see your good works, and glorify your Father which is in Heaven."* (Matthew 5:16 KJV)

MEDITATIONS

_____

_____

_____

_____

_____

_____

_____

_____

_____

_____

_____

_____

_____

DAY
29

"Then He called His twelve disciples together and gave them power and authority over all devils, and to cure diseases."

—Luke 1:9

We are Spirit beings and are constantly living in Spiritual warfare. Ephesians six says *"For we wrestle not against flesh and blood, but against the rulers of darkness of this world, against Spiritual wickedness in high places."* (V.12 KJV)

Everything that comes against us that is not good, or of God, is either, a direct result of our own bad decisions, or the powers of darkness at work. However, just like the disciples, we have been given authority through Jesus Christ and His blood shed at Calvary's cross, over the powers of darkness, as well as, the authority to lay hands on people and see them healed. Have you ever gone through a season where the enemy attacked you from every angle? Those days when the enemy is putting thoughts in your mind nonstop or causing you to worry about things that are most likely never going to happen.

James says, to, *"Resist the devil and he will flee from you."* (4:7 KJV) The next time the enemy is coming at you relentlessly, do what Jesus did, remind him that you, *"Do not live by bread alone, but by every word that proceeds out of the mouth of God."* (Matthew 4:4 KJV) Be encouraged today knowing that you are not just starting another day, but you are starting your day with authority given to you by God through His son Jesus Christ. Go out today and conquer all that awaits you. You have got this, in Jesus name!

MEDITATIONS

_____

_____

_____

_____

_____

_____

_____

_____

_____

_____

_____

_____

_____

_____

DAY

30

"The Spirit of the Lord is upon me because He has anointed me to preach the gospel to the poor; He has sent me to heal the broken hearted, to preach deliverance to the captives, and recovering of sight to the blind, to set at liberty them who are bruised."

—Luke 4:18

I would be remiss as I finish this book not to address the subject of abuse, whether it be physical, emotional, or sexual, it can leave a scar deep within the heart. Overcoming the pain can seem impossible, but its not. There is an answer. If you have suffered abuse at the hands of another, I want you to know that Jesus paid a great price at Calvary for you to be healed, made whole, and set free from the pain you carry.

I recently preached a message, titled *'Bruised, but not defeated.'* In my message I brought out the fact that although you may have been hurt in the cruelest way—bruised—crushed, you do not have to live a defeated life. You can live a life of Victory found only in Christ Jesus.

Many people today suffer from anxiety and depression that can be linked to abuse suffered as a child or maybe even as an adult through the act of Domestic Violence. There is a Spirit behind what they are feeling, and it can be identified as a Spirit of fear and torment. As the person is tormented, it can cause physical problems such as heart disease, headaches, muscle aches, digestive problems, and fatigue. In addition, they may be easily distracted, or maintain a negative attitude about virtually everything.

People who have been bruised, or carry an emotional scar unfortunately often feel hopeless—even Christians. Jesus did not shed His blood at Calvary for you to walk around defeated and feeling hopeless. He gave His life that you may be set free from the bondage of darkness that accompanies years of abuse. Isaiah tells us that, *"He was wounded for our transgressions, He was bruised for our iniquities, the chastisment of our peace was upon Him and with His stripes we are healed."* (53:5 KJV)

If you are reading this and it applies to you, say this prayer, and believe God for your deliverance today. Today is your day to be set free.

Dear God in Heaven,

I humble myself before you today as I come to you with a heavy and broken heart, a wounded Spirit and troubled emotions that I cannot change. Lord I thank you for your son and the price He paid for me at Calvary. I thank you for your promises to me and remind you that your word says you are my healer, deliverer, and restorer. Father I ask you today to help me to forgive my abuser, and to remove every hurt, all depression and anxiety and negative thought. Lord take my thoughts captive today, bringing them into obedience with you. Restore back to me all that the enemy has stolen through abuse and strengthen me to keep going, to share my testimony of your goodness and to be a blessing to others going through what you have brought me out of. In Jesus Name. Amen

MEDITATIONS

_____

_____

_____

_____

_____

_____

_____

_____

_____

_____

_____

_____

_____

_____

DAY

31

"For whatsoever things were written aforetime were written for our learning that we through patience and comfort of the scriptures might have hope."

—Romans 15:4

We live in perilous and uncertain times; it can be difficult to look past the hardships we endure in daily life and see the light at the end of the tunnel. It is crucial to remember that we serve a God of hope. He is our hope and the one we place our Faith in. Romans 15:13 says, *"Now the God of hope fill you with all joy, and peace in believing, that you may abound in Hope, through the power of the Holy Spirit."*

To obtain this we must keep our faith anchored in Christ, no matter what comes our way. We should not be caught off guard by events unfolding before us. The word tells us, *"This know also, that in the last days perilous times shall come."* (II Timothy 3:1 KJV) *"For men shall be lovers of their ownselves, coveteous, boasters, proud, blasphemers, disobedient to parents, unthankful, unholy."* (v.2) This is an accurate description of the times we are currently living in, but in the midst of it all, we still have a hope, because scripture also tells us that, *"when we see these things, we are to look up, for our redemption draweth nigh."* (Luke 21:28 KJV) The greatest promise of all, is Jesus Christ coming for us, to carry us home!

I Thessalonians 4:16-19 says, *"For the Lord himself shall descend from Heaven with a shout, with the voice of the Archangel and the trump of God: and the dead in Christ shall rise first." "Then we which are alive and remain shall be caught up together with them in the clouds to meet the Lord in the air and so shall we ever be with the Lord."* We have a hope and so much to look forward to. Soon we are leaving this sin cursed world! Be encouraged today to hold on to the hand of the one who is our blessed hope and on His way; to carry us home. Hold on! Jesus is coming!

MEDITATIONS

_____

_____

_____

_____

_____

_____

_____

_____

_____

_____

_____

_____

PRAYER FOR
SALVATION

*"That at the time you were without Christ
being aliens from the commonwealth of Israel,
and strangers from the covenants of promise,
having no hope, and without God in the
world."*

—Ephesians 2:12

If you read this book and you do not know the Lord Jesus
Christ as your Lord and Savior, then today can be your day
to step out of the darkness, and into the light. All you have
to do, is say the prayer below and believe it with your whole
heart. Jesus will meet you right where you are, and your
world can forever be changed.

*Dear God in Heaven, I come to you today
as lost sinner in need of a Savior. I am
asking that you save my soul and cleanse me
from all sin. I realize in my heart my need
of Salvation, which can only come through*

Christ Jesus. I am accepting Christ into my heart and what He did on the Cross in order to purchase my redemption. In obedience to your word, I confess with my mouth the Lord Jesus, and believe in my heart that God has raised Him from the dead. You have said in your word that whosoever calls on the name of the Lord will be saved. I have called upon your name as you have said, and I believe that right now, I am saved.

ABOUT THE AUTHOR

A current resident of Gates County, North Carolina, Connie Smithson also worked in the Rural County for many years as a CPS Investigator/ Social Worker and Domestic Violence advocate. She graduated from College of the Albemarle with an Associates of Arts Degree, as well as Elizabeth City State University, with a Bachelor of Science degree in Criminal Justice. After completing her Bachelor of Science degree, Connie went on to obtain her Master's degree in Criminal Justice at Kaplan University. Today, Connie has dedicated her life to serving God wherever He leads and is available to speak as the opportunities become available. Connie can be contacted by email at quietmoments08@yahoo.com.

Printed in the United States
by Baker & Taylor Publisher Services